'Laughter is timeless, imagination has no age and dreams are forever' - Walt Disney

A child's imagination knows no boundaries. Children have an innate ability to imagine and create stories from scratch and are always looking for new ideas and experiences to understand the world around them.

These "Which Would You Choose? – Awesome & unusual Superpowers Edition" questions will stimulate your kids' imagination and bring out some amazingly insightful, funny and interesting answers.

This book is a great tool to :

• **Improve communication** by encouraging your children to talk and express themselves freely while discussing their choices in a fun and light-hearted way.

• **Encourage critical thinking** : these questions will help children develop hypotheses about the different scenarios and encourage them to think in new and different ways.

• **Stimulate imagination and creative thinking** through our list of ridiculous and original superpowers and abilities !

• **Strengthen relationships** by spurring healthy and interactive discussion in a fun and care-free environment.

• **Nurture curiosity and improve general knowledge** with our list of Trivia questions and answers.

These questions are an excellent idea to get the conversation started!

Welcome !

Thank you for purchasing my book!

My name is Mirabelle, I'm an indie author and a full time parent.
I've been working on creating fun and educational games, stories and books for kids for the past 12 years.

As a parent of two, finding ways to entertain the kids while teaching them how to think, communicate and learn important values has been one of my top priorities.
Developing curiosity and creative imagination has become crucial to adapt and grow in today's society.

I really hope you enjoy this book, and if you do, please consider leaving us a review sharing your experience, I'd love to read it and I'd really appreciate it!

Meet Zippo !

He is one little troublesome clown.
Zippo is a tricky little brat known for his high energy and his endless pranks.

Zippo loves to break the rules when he gets bored, but it ends up getting him into a lot of trouble. He goes on many crazy and wild adventures with his best companion and friend, Dolly the dog.

Despite his irresponsibly playful and mischievous behavior, Zippo is a kind-hearted clown, has a great sense of humor, boundless curiosity, imagination and excitement about life !

How to Play ?

- The objective of the game is to decide between dilemmas, then speculate and vote on the choices of others.
- **Play with minimum two players** - If you have a large group of people, you can play around in a circle or even form teams.

- **At the beginning of each round, decide on who's going to be the first player** - who will read aloud the first dilemma.

- The second player must think carefully and choose **only one answer,** without revealing their choice.

- Now, the first player will have to guess which answer the second player has chosen. If their guess is correct, they score one point.

- The second player will have to **explain his choice !**

- Make sure to keep scores and decide on a prize or a challenge for each round !

Most importantly, have fun, laugh and enjoy your time with your family and loved ones!

Round 1

WOULD YOU RATHER ?

Make animal sounds whenever you want to talk or... have leaves for your hair?

GUESS POINT: __/1

GUESS POINT: __/1

Have a nose that's shaped like a candy cane or... a nose that's shaped like a banana?

WOULD YOU RATHER ?

PLAYER 1

Have to sleep in a trash can
or...
sleep upside down like a bat?

GUESS POINT: __/1

GUESS POINT: __/1

PLAYER 2

Only be able to crawl everywhere like a worm
or...
walk everywhere like a gorilla?

WOULD YOU RATHER ?

Have two extra fingers that you can climb walls with

or...

two fewer toes and you can jump like a frog?

GUESS POINT: __/1

GUESS POINT: __/1

Only be able to whisper very softly

or...

shout as loud as you can?

WOULD YOU RATHER ?

Eat a whole lemon that turns you yellow for two days
or...
a teaspoonful of salt that makes you thirsty for a whole week?

GUESS POINT: __/1

GUESS POINT: __/1

be able to breathe under water
or...
have the power to manipulate any form of technology?

WOULD YOU RATHER ?

Turn invisible every time you burp
or...
have super strength every time you fart?

GUESS POINT: __/1

GUESS POINT: __/1

Be able to play only one song on every instrument
or...
be able to say only one sentence in every language?

Round 2

WOULD YOU RATHER ?

PLAYER 1

Have feet twice as big and be unable to wear shoes
or...
feet half as small and only be able to wear pink slippers?

GUESS POINT: __/1

GUESS POINT: __/1

PLAYER 2

Always have to shout your name when you enter a room
or...
always bunny hop when you leave a room?

WOULD YOU RATHER ?

PLAYER 1

Have a pet dragon the size of a hamster
or...
a pet hamster the size of a dragon?

GUESS POINT: __/1

GUESS POINT: __/1

PLAYER 2

Drink a whole glass of hot sauce and be able to breathe fire
or...
eat a whole jar of mayonnaise and be able to turn things to ice?

WOULD YOU RATHER ?

have the ability to breath fire out of your mouth
or...
be able to control water & wind?

GUESS POINT: __/1

GUESS POINT: __/1

Kiss a toad that turns into your crush
or...
hug a cactus that turns into your favorite celebrity?

WOULD YOU RATHER ?

Randomly turn into a mouse for one day every month or...
randomly turn into an eagle for one day every week?

GUESS POINT: __/1

GUESS POINT: __/1

Have a square head that can break through concrete or...
have a balloon head but be super smart?

WOULD YOU RATHER ?

Ride a T-Rex to school every day
or...
fly on a pterodactyl to school every day?

GUESS POINT: __/1

GUESS POINT: __/1

be able to understand anything without the need of studying it
or...
to tell the future and see the past of any person?

Round 3

WOULD YOU RATHER ?

Eat cake every day and grow five pant sizes or... eat vegetables every day and always need to fart?

GUESS POINT: __/1

GUESS POINT: __/1

Only wear shoes made from bricks that get heavier with every step or... pants made from newspapers that tear with every step?

19

WOULD YOU RATHER ?

Smell like stinky cheese and be chased by mice
Or...
smell like steamed cabbage and be chased by ducks?

GUESS POINT: __/1

GUESS POINT: __/1

Only be able to eat green food and get super speed
or...
only be able to eat red food and get super strength?

20

WOULD YOU RATHER ?

Eat snails for lunch every day
Or...
eat sardines for lunch every day?

GUESS POINT: __/1

GUESS POINT: __/1

Fart every time you sit down
Or...
burp every time you raise your arms?

WOULD YOU RATHER ?

have the ability to acquire information during your sleep or...
be able to take photos at will just by blinking your eyes and store them in your mind?

GUESS POINT: __/1

GUESS POINT: __/1

Have an itchy butt every day but you can only scratch it once Or...
be ticklish whenever someone touches you and you're a people magnet?

WOULD YOU RATHER ?

Smell like onions every day and make people cry when you're around

or...

have big yellow teeth and make people laugh whenever you're around?

GUESS POINT: __/1

GUESS POINT: __/1

Sleep in a stable for one night

or...

cuddle a skunk for one hour?

Round 4

WOULD YOU RATHER ?

have to ability to manipulate the smell of anything/anyone
or...
to eat anything and to transform it into gold?

GUESS POINT: __/1

GUESS POINT: __/1

Sweat pickle juice that attracts a lot of flies
or...
sweat sour milk that attracts a lot of cows?

WOULD YOU RATHER ?

Have an alien friend with a laser blaster

or...

a time-traveling friend who can ride dinosaurs?

GUESS POINT: __/1

GUESS POINT: __/1

Have a dog that always farts

or...

a cat that always burps?

26

WOULD YOU RATHER ?

> *Kiss a smelly zombie and become a zombie*
> *Or...*
> *hug a dusty mummy and sneeze every hour for the rest of your life?*

GUESS POINT: __/1

GUESS POINT: __/1

> *have the power to decide the winner of any game*
> *or...*
> *be able to create a copy of yourself and become invisible?*

WOULD YOU RATHER ?

Be bald but you can never wear a hat
or...
be covered in hair from head to toe but you can never wear underwear?

PLAYER 1

GUESS POINT: __/1

GUESS POINT: __/1

PLAYER 2

be able to turn into an ice dragon
or...
a majestic unicorn?

WOULD YOU RATHER ?

have the power to gain an animal's abilities by touching it

or...

the ability to transform anyone into a monkey for one day ?

GUESS POINT: __/1

GUESS POINT: __/1

Hop everywhere like a bunny and only be able to eat carrots

or...

roll everywhere like an armadillo and only be able to eat bugs?

29

Round 5

WOULD YOU RATHER ?

Wear clown makeup every day
or...
leave a trail of fairy glitter wherever you go?

GUESS POINT: __/1

GUESS POINT: __/1

Have a nose the size of an eggplant that can smell for miles
or...
ears the size of dinner plates that can pick up radio signals?

WOULD YOU RATHER ?

PLAYER 1

Have a big red pimple on your forehead that can talk
or...
a massive booger hanging out of your nose that points toward food for the rest of your life?

GUESS POINT: __/1

GUESS POINT: __/1

PLAYER 2

Go to school in boxers but your butt is showing
or...
go to school in fluffy pink unicorn pajamas?

WOULD YOU RATHER ?

*Eat broccoli every day for the rest of your life and turn green like the Hulk
or...
eat boogers for a month and become strong whenever you eat them?*

GUESS POINT: __/1

GUESS POINT: __/1

*have the power to generate electricity from your body
or...
the ability to recreate anything you have touched?*

33

WOULD YOU RATHER ?

PLAYER 1

Never be able to play video games ever again
or...
be forced to run to school every day for a month?

GUESS POINT: __/1

GUESS POINT: __/1

PLAYER 2

Have a monkey tail that you can climb with
or...
a pig nose that you can find anything with?

Round 6

WOULD YOU RATHER ?

PLAYER 1

> be able to create cure for any illness
> or...
> have the ability to make hilarious jokes and pranks all the time?

GUESS POINT: __/1

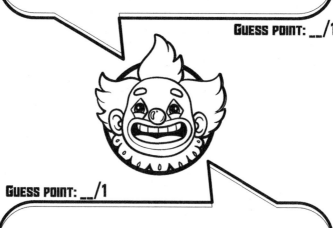

GUESS POINT: __/1

PLAYER 2

> Kiss a snake and it bites your nose
> or...
> pet a jellyfish and it stings your butt?

WOULD YOU RATHER ?

PLAYER 1

Lick the bottom of your shoe and get unlimited candy
or...
lick the bathroom floor and get unlimited video games?

GUESS POINT: __/1

GUESS POINT: __/1

PLAYER 2

be able to bounce like a rubber ball
or...
to grow and have a second head?

WOULD YOU RATHER ?

Eat a dead beetle for breakfast every morning for a week
or...
eat a live earthworm for dessert every night for a week?

GUESS POINT: __/1

GUESS POINT: __/1

have the power to pull things into any direction
or...
discover and store people's secrets in a book?

WOULD YOU RATHER ?

Sneeze chocolate-flavored
boogers
or...
cry strawberry-flavored tears?

GUESS POINT: __/1

GUESS POINT: __/1

Be two feet tall and be able
to talk to animals
or...
eight feet tall and be able
to fly but only for five
minutes every day?

39

Round 7

WOULD YOU RATHER ?

have the power to give the best hugs ever
or...
be able to hold breath as long as you want?

GUESS POINT: __/1

GUESS POINT: __/1

Be a poor astronaut that can fly anywhere in space
or...
be a rich janitor that can never eat candy or ice cream?

WOULD YOU RATHER ?

Speak in front of the whole
school for five minutes
or...
work in the school cafeteria
for a whole month?

GUESS POINT: __/1

GUESS POINT: __/1

Have a bee sting you on the
butt
or...
hold a snake for two minutes?

42

WOULD YOU RATHER ?

Have a beard that can arm wrestle people
or...
no eyebrows but you can see for very long distances?

GUESS POINT: __/1

GUESS POINT: __/1

have the power to make anyone copy your movements
or...
make everything you touch excessively cute?

43

WOULD YOU RATHER ?

Have seaweed for hair and you can breathe underwater
or...
tentacles for feet and you can swim super fast?

GUESS POINT: __/1

GUESS POINT: __/1

Wear glasses for your whole life and have blindingly white teeth
or...
wear braces for five years and have microscopic vision?

Round 8

WOULD YOU RATHER ?

Have a squeaky voice for a month and become a famous singer
or...
not be able to talk for a week and have superpowers?

GUESS POINT: __/1

GUESS POINT: __/1

Spend summer vacation exploring a rainforest and find a lost civilization
or...
climb a snowy mountain and find bigfoot

WOULD YOU RATHER ?

Eat candy that tastes like puke and makes you super smart

or...

eat puke that tastes like candy but you fail your next test?

GUESS POINT: __/1

GUESS POINT: __/1

have the ability to make people sing any song you want

or...

to create and control the clouds in the sky?

WOULD YOU RATHER ?

PLAYER 1

> *Go to school in your mom's dress and everyone says it suits you*
> *or...*
> *go to school in your dad's boxers and you get detention?*

GUESS POINT: __/1

GUESS POINT: __/1

PLAYER 2

> *have the ability to see in the dark*
> *or...*
> *to communicate with anyone around the world using your mind?*

WOULD YOU RATHER ?

Grow up 20 years right now and be a garbage man or... stay this age forever and become a scientist?

GUESS POINT: __/1

GUESS POINT: __/1

the ability to transform partially or fully into a giant spider or... a giant mantis?

Round 9

WOULD YOU RATHER ?

Walk around in a flamingo suit that squawks with every step
or...
fart loudly in public and set off the smoke alarms?

GUESS POINT: __/1

GUESS POINT: __/1

have the ability to shrink any object into a toy size
or...
be able to hold in your own burps and farts for unlimited time?

WOULD YOU RATHER ?

> *Eat a hot dog that tastes like feet*
> *or...*
> *feet that taste like hot dogs?*

GUESS POINT: __/1

GUESS POINT: __/1

> *Play outside with your friends and save the neighborhood from aliens*
> *or...*
> *play video games inside alone and save the city from robots?*

WOULD YOU RATHER ?

Get chased by an elephant-sized bunny that wants to eat your pants

or...

get chased by 50 bunny-sized elephants that want to nibble on your toes?

GUESS POINT: __/1

GUESS POINT: __/1

Never eat your favorite meal again but you can have 10 of every type of candy

or...

only eat your favorite meal but you can have as much as you could ever want?

WOULD YOU RATHER ?

PLAYER 1

Only live in a hot area and always feel cold
or...
only live where it snows but always feel hot?

GUESS POINT: __/1

GUESS POINT: __/1

PLAYER 2

Stub your toe every day but the rest of you is invincible
or...
drop your pencil in every class but get straight A's?

Round 10

WOULD YOU RATHER ?

have the ability to put anyone to sleep with the snap of a finger

or...

to generate smoothies of any flavor?

GUESS POINT: __/1

GUESS POINT: __/1

Be the fastest person on earth but you're a giant snail

or...

be able to fly but you're a tiny pigeon?

WOULD YOU RATHER ?

PLAYER 1

have the ability to control
other people's hands
or...
the power to create magical
toys?

GUESS POINT: __/1

GUESS POINT: __/1

PLAYER 2

Swim in a pool of pudding but
you have to eat it all with a
teaspoon afterward
or...
build a snowman from ice cream
but you have to lick it all up like
a lollipop?

WOULD YOU RATHER ?

PLAYER 1

> Read minds but all the thoughts are in another language
> or...
> be able to teleport anywhere within one foot?

GUESS POINT: __/1

GUESS POINT: __/1

PLAYER 2

> Moo like a cow and control cows every time you drink milk
> or...
> cluck like a chicken and command an army of chickens every time you eat eggs?

WOULD YOU RATHER ?

have the power to regrow and shape your teeth
or...
manipulate your hair and have total control over it?

GUESS POINT: __/1

GUESS POINT: __/1

Have three arms but you can't control what they pick up
or...
three legs but you can't control where they walk?

Round 11

WOULD YOU RATHER ?

Only be able to walk around in your underwear for the rest of your life
or...
walk around in winter clothes all summer?

GUESS POINT: __/1

GUESS POINT: __/1

Discover a living dinosaur but he's very angry
or...
discover a lost pirate treasure but it's haunted by pirate ghosts?

WOULD YOU RATHER ?

PLAYER 1

Never need to brush your teeth again but you stink like gym socks

or...

never need to wash again but your breath smells like garlic?

GUESS POINT: __/1

GUESS POINT: __/1

PLAYER 2

have the power to hear anything from a far distance

or...

the ability to enter an other person's dreams?

WOULD YOU RATHER ?

Be friends with Batman but have to fight the Avengers
or...
be friends with Iron Man but have to fight the Justice League?

GUESS POINT: __/1

GUESS POINT: __/1

Go on the world's tallest roller coaster and throw up on your crush
or...
go down the world's fastest water slide naked?

WOULD YOU RATHER ?

> *Every time you stand you need to do a little dance or...*
> *every time you sit you announce very loudly that you've sat down?*

GUESS POINT: __/1

GUESS POINT: __/1

> *Never need to do homework again but only get straight C's or...*
> *never need to do gym again but all your clothes become too small for you?*

WOULD YOU RATHER ?

be a famous actor that
always plays the nerd
or...
a rock star that only sings
in gibberish?

GUESS POINT: __/1

GUESS POINT: __/1

have the power to reverse
time
or...
the ability to climb and
crawl walls?

Round 12

WOULD YOU RATHER ?

have the power to bring objects to life

or...

have superhuman endurance and never get tired?

GUESS POINT: __/1

GUESS POINT: __/1

PLAYER 2

Have your own movie theater that only plays Barbie films

or...

your own arcade room that only has chess games?

WOULD YOU RATHER ?

the ability to silence babies whenever they start crying
or...
to never ever need to go to the bathroom?

GUESS POINT: __/1

GUESS POINT: __/1

Have every vegetable taste like candy
or...
have water taste like your favorite soda?

WOULD YOU RATHER ?

the power the bring
anything you draw into life
or...
the ability to always say
the right thing?

GUESS POINT: __/1

GUESS POINT: __/1

have the ability to make
people dance every
time you sneeze
or...
rolling on the floor every time
you clap?

WOULD YOU RATHER ?

> have the ability to be best
> friend with every person
> you encounter
> or...
> the power to make anything
> you want to do permissible?

GUESS POINT: __/1

GUESS POINT: __/1

> the power to always have
> what you need in your pockets
> or...
> the ability to have a second
> chance every time you do
> something wrong?

WOULD YOU RATHER ?

Be a world-class athlete but you can only play a sport that you hate
or...
be a water boy for your favorite team?

GUESS POINT: __/1

GUESS POINT: __/1

Have to suck on your dirty socks every morning for a month
or...
have to eat your least favorite vegetable with every meal for a year?

Round 13

WOULD YOU RATHER ?

Have your laughs sound like farts for a year
or...
only be able to speak French for two months?

GUESS POINT: __/1

GUESS POINT: __/1

have the ability to set different saving points in your life to which you can return to
or...
the power to memorize every book you read?

WOULD YOU RATHER ?

> *Have 1,000 ants in your pants and you can only get rid of them by breakdancing in public*
> *or...*
> *have 1,000 ants wearing pants march through your bedroom?*

GUESS POINT: __/1

GUESS POINT: __/1

> *have the ability to turn your fingers into pens/pencils*
> *or...*
> *the ability to cry tears of your favorite juice?*

WOULD YOU RATHER ?

PLAYER 1

> *Train an angry beaver to grow trees*
> *or...*
> *train a grumpy pig to not roll in the mud?*

GUESS POINT: __/1

GUESS POINT: __/1

PLAYER 2

> *Ride Pegasus, but he farts rainbows to school every day*
> *or...*
> *ride a giant turtle and only get there an hour late?*

WOULD YOU RATHER ?

PLAYER 1

Be constantly sticky and bees are attracted to you
or...
be constantly itchy and mosquitoes are attracted to you?

GUESS POINT: __/1

GUESS POINT: __/1

PLAYER 2

Have fingers that squeak every time you touch something
or...
feet that honk whenever you walk?

WOULD YOU RATHER ?

Pee your pants once a year in front of your whole school Or...
pee your pants once a week in front of your family?

GUESS POINT: __/1

GUESS POINT: __/1

have the ability to tolerate extremely high or low temperatures
or...
the power to be able to do homework when you're asleep?

Round 14

WOULD YOU RATHER ?

PLAYER 1

Live in a glass house and always have to be naked
or...
live in a house with no windows that smells like an armpit?

GUESS POINT: __/1

GUESS POINT: __/1

PLAYER 2

Lose a few hairs every time you win at a game
or...
a finger or toe grows an inch every time you lose?

WOULD YOU RATHER ?

PLAYER 1

> Be able to do everything amazingly but only for 10 minutes a day
> or...
> be somewhat okay at everything but only on Mondays?

GUESS POINT: __/1

GUESS POINT: __/1

PLAYER 2

> Everything you dream at night comes true when you wake up
> or...
> everything a random person dreams at night comes true in your room when you wake up?

WOULD YOU RATHER ?

Be able to fly, but only if you shout all your secrets at the top of your lungs

or...

be able to run fast but only while holding your breath?

GUESS POINT: __/1

GUESS POINT: __/1

Have to breathe in and out through your eyes

or...

taste everything you eat and drink through your ears?

WOULD YOU RATHER ?

PLAYER 1

Wear old-timey cowboy clothes to school for a year or...
wear a metal box with flashing lights to school for a year?

GUESS POINT: __/1

GUESS POINT: __/1

PLAYER 2

Eat soup with chopsticks for every breakfast or...
eat steak with a spoon for every dinner?

WOULD YOU RATHER ?

Have to wind up your legs like a toy car every time you want to run

or...

have to power your arms with AA batteries?

GUESS POINT: __/1

GUESS POINT: __/1

have the ability to transform your body into someone else's

or...

have to ability to control someone's else mood?

Final Round

WOULD YOU RATHER ?

Become your favorite superhero every weekend
or...
be an all-powerful wizard but only after bedtime?

GUESS POINT: __/1

GUESS POINT: __/1

have the ability to master any skill/tool you need
or...
the power to be present in many places at once?

WOULD YOU RATHER ?

PLAYER 1

> *Live in a mansion that changes color every day and smells like old lady perfume or...*
> *live in a normal house that has no TV, computer, or video games?*

GUESS POINT: __/1

GUESS POINT: __/1

PLAYER 2

> *have the ability to fly but only when you're inside an airplane or...*
> *the ability to slow down time but only during video games loading screens?*

WOULD YOU RATHER ?

have the ability to create snowballs out of thin air or...
have the magical power to always be on time?

GUESS POINT: __/1

GUESS POINT: __/1

have the ability to watch your favorite show/movie just by closing your eyes or...
the power to be incredibly accurate whenever you throw anything?

WOULD YOU RATHER ?

Say all sentences backward for a year
or...
talk through charades for a month?

GUESS POINT: __/1

GUESS POINT: __/1

Have one eye in the middle of your head that can see through walls
or...
have two mouths that can speak every language?

WOULD YOU RATHER ?

Have to chew on uncooked rice every day for a week
or...
have to eat cold anchovies for breakfast every day for a month?

GUESS POINT: __/1

GUESS POINT: __/1

the ability to summon your hand shadow puppets
or...
or the power of unbreakable bones?

Congratulations !

You succeeded at this ridiculous decision making challenge !

I hope you had a fun time playing this game. If you enjoyed this book, I would really appreciate if you leave us a review sharing your experience and stories. **_It would mean a lot !_**

If you haven't done so already, make sure to check out my other books and follow my author's page on Amazon for future releases !

Till next time,
Mirabelle.

Riddle Quest
BONUS ACCESS

Join our fun club and get bonus monthly access to our giveaways & extras !

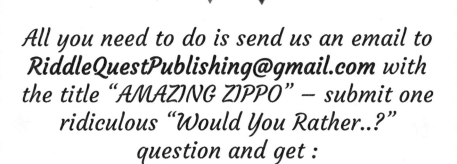

All you need to do is send us an email to *RiddleQuestPublishing@gmail.com* with the title *"AMAZING ZIPPO"* – submit one ridiculous *"Would You Rather..?"* question and get :

- An entry to our monthly giveaway to win **50$ Amazon Gift Card** !

- Access to our **free extras** !

A winner with the best submission will be picked each month and will be contacted via email.

Best of Luck !

Printed in Great Britain
by Amazon

79736613R20058